WHERE IT AL

THE 1978 HAWAIIAN

IRON MAN TRIATHLON

TOM KNOLL

Where It All Began:

The 1978 Hawaiian Iron Man Triathlon

By

Tom Knoll, USMC, Ret.

2014

ISBN:0615976646
ISBN-13:978-0615976648

Edited and Formatted by
Gordon P. Foreman
gpforeman@gmail.com

DEDICATION

I dedicate this book to Gordon Haller, John Dunbar, Dave Orlowski, Ian Emberson, Sterling Lewis, Henry Forrest, Frank Day, John Collins, Archie Hapai, Dan Hendrickson, Harold (Butch) Irving, John Lloyd, John King, Ralph Yawata, along with myself (The Class of 1978). It was a thrill being a part of it with all of you.

As a Marine Korean and Vietnam veteran, and an Afghanistan and Iraq veteran with the Defense Intelligence Agency, I would also like to dedicate this book to the troops, the men and women who are putting everything else on hold to defend our country in Afghanistan and everywhere else in the world on land, sea and in the air. You are the cream of the crop and hopefully the leaders of our country in years to come.

"*Tom Knoll...Legs of Iron, Heart of Gold*."-
Marine Officers Wives Club

"***Thanks for Paving the Way for the Rest of Us to Follow***"-Paula Newby-Fraser, 8-time Professional Female Ironman Triathlon World Championship Winner.

"***You can keep going and your legs might hurt for a week or you can quit and your mind will hurt for a lifetime***"-Mark Allen, 6-time Professional Male Ironman Triathlon World Championship Winner

CONTENTS

INTRODUCTION

Somewhere around 2004, there was an effort to get each of the original 1978 Hawaii Iron Men to write a chapter in a book that was planned to be titled, "Ironman: The Untold Story". This was also to include data on how the Ironman came to be. I was in charge of coordinating all this and I thought it would be an easy, fun chore. Not quite.

Some showed interest, with one or two of them writing their chapter. Others said they were very busy but said they would write a chapter when they had some free time. One person said he was not interested and several I was unable to contact. Pete Adams and his wife Robin, along with myself, had put in a considerable amount of time and effort to try to make this book a reality. The bottom line was there would not be a book written by all of us. We had already lost one of our original Ironmen, Henry Forrest, to pancreatic cancer, in 2008. He was one of the few who had written his chapter. So here's the fact. Time flies. Too much time had already passed since our plan to write the book back in 2004. Based on our experiences and research, we believed that there was an amazing amount of information about the first Ironman that people would find very interesting, and much of it had never been published.

Closing on the age of 81, here's my version, in a book titled, "***Where It All Began***". Along with the details of the original Ironman in 1978, people want to know what I have done in the 35 years since then. So this is also included.

To start out, over the years I have amassed a huge amount of material on what took place in the 1978 Ironman. This includes newspaper and magazine articles, some photos, plus chats with a few of the other original Iron Men over the years. The material was stored in one of my closets in a packing box almost too heavy to pick up. Thank God I am a packrat! My task was to go through every article from all the 35 years of written material and find any information on the 1978 Iron Man Triathlon, and note it down. This provided me with several 10-hour days, and I found a lot of interesting things that you readers should know about.

If you go along with "don't believe

everything you read in the newspaper," you will appreciate that some things printed were right on, some were partially wrong, and some were totally wrong. Along with this, some of the information might be wrong without you knowing it.

Here are a few of the many, many examples of common misinformation about the 1978 Hawaii Ironman:

1. Twelve of us completed the 1978 Hawaii Ironman. Right! Not 11 or 13.

2. Gordon Haller was not a former Marine. He was officer in the Navy Reserve.

3. Some naval officers got drunk in a bar in downtown Honolulu and came up with the Ironman idea. Wrong!

4. John Collins "breached the idea" at a

Waikiki swim club banquet. Wrong! He did breach the idea, but not there.

5. This was the first triathlon ever. Wrong! More details on the early history of the triathlon concept will be discussed in Chapter 10.

What I am getting around to is some information that I am quoting and including in the book could be challenged. Great! Charge on! I would love to hear your version.

There is an old saying, "I may not agree with what you say, but I'll defend to my death your right to say it." Tom Knoll's version: You may not agree with what I say, but I'll defend to your death your right to say it.

So here's the good news: Pete Adams and I have teamed up to put out this book, "***Where It***

All Began" and a portion of the proceeds from each book will go to charity.

Writing the book has created a lot of great memories. Creating the 1978 part was a whole lot easier than re-creating the last 35 years of my life. I was the oldest person competing in 1978, a 46-year old active duty Marine. Add 35 years to that, and you get 81. It's tough trying to remember everything, but I think you get the idea.

Enjoy the book. I hope you have many rainbows and keep living your dreams. I'm sure living mine with many more to come.

CHAPTER 1
PRIMO GARDENS - THE PLACE WHERE IT BEGAN...

It was early December 1977, and I was at the awards ceremony for the Oahu 134.6-mile Around The Island Team Perimeter Relay Race with seven members on each team. The ceremony was being held at Primo Gardens, which is near Pearl City on the island of Oahu. The awards ceremony was being sponsored by The Primo Brewing & Malting Company and they were graciously offering free Primo Beer to a couple of hundred athletes in attendance.

I was standing at a table enjoying a cool

Primo beer where a group of us including John Collins and Dan Hendrickson were talking about how we did at the relay race and the upcoming Honolulu Marathon. Soon a friendly discussion broke out about what type of endurance athletes were the most fit.

John believed that cyclist were the most fit after reading an article about Eddy Merckx in Sports Illustrated. Others debated that ultra endurance runners had the highest level of fitness, while others disagreed and said that long distance swimmers were the fittest. John then asked one of the swimmers in the group what the most challenging swimming event was on Oahu. The response from the swimmer was "the 2.4 mile open ocean Waikiki Roughwater Swim". John made a mental note of this and I felt something was forming in his mind.

A short time later he asked a runner who was also a cyclist, what the most challenging bike event was on the Island? He responded "the 112 mile Dick Evans Around the Island Bike Race". (Note although the circumference of the Island is roughly 136 miles, there is a part of that called Kaena Point which was not part of the Around the Island Bike Race as there are no roads there and totally unbikeable.) No one had mentioned the fact to John or any of us that the Bike Race was actually a two day event!

With John now in charge of the conversation, I had no doubt that he had something on his mind. He finally got to the bottom line and suggested we should come up with a "triathlon" and combine the 2.4 mile Roughwater Swim, the 112 mile Dick Evans

Around the Island Race, along with the 26.2 mile Honolulu Marathon as one event and try to complete all three of the events within 24 hours. We naturally thought that he was kidding or that he had taken leave of his senses.

When the band that was playing background music took a break, John jumped up on stage and grabbed the microphone announcing that he was putting on a new triathlon combining all three events "and that anyone who could do this would be called an Iron Man and would have bragging rights for the rest of their lives!" He got a good laugh from some of the crowd but others shook their heads in amazement and total disbelief at what John had just announced.

John got off the stage and returned to the table. We really weren't sure if he was serious about the triathlon idea or not. As a group we all discussed it, but none of us really thought that anyone could possibly complete all the events in one day. Although it was a wild idea, it was also very tempting. I thought the idea floated somewhere between total insanity and something neat, leaning a little towards the latter.

The next morning I woke up and wondered if this all was one of my wilder dreams. It made me think of a line from the poet Edgar Allan Poe who wrote "***Dreaming dreams no mortal ever dared to dream before***."

CHAPTER 2
MAKING THE DECISION

The morning following the awards ceremony at Primo Gardens, I went into work and ran into Cpl. Dave Orlowski. Dave was a fellow Marine who was also at the awards ceremony the previous evening. We talked about the proposed triathlon, and kidding him I said that "I was putting him in it". Dave looked a little bit mystified when I said that, but he also looked like he was seriously considering doing it. After that Dave began to try to recruit Marine Cpl. John Loyd, who also seemed interested in the prospect of doing it.

A few days later, I got a call from John Collins. He wanted to know if I was going to participate in the triathlon that he now planned on putting on. I told him that I would need a couple of days to think it over. A fellow marathoner told me "I don't think that anyone could finish it, but if anyone could it would be you."

It was time to weigh everything on the scales of both negative and positive aspects and to make a decision as to whether or not I was going to attempt this seemingly impossible physical challenge. For sure I was already losing a lot of sleep over this.

On the negative side of the scale was the fact that I had a full time job as the

Counterintelligence Representative for the Kaneohe Bay Marine Corps Air Station. If the challenge was accepted, I would only be able to train in the three disciplines during non-working hours. Another item for the negative side of the scale was the fact that I had not ridden a bike since I was a paper boy delivering The Milwaukee Journal, and that was over 30 years ago. Adding more to the negative side, was the fact that the last real swimming I had done was during my five year tour in Marine Recon where I attended the demanding three week US Navy Underwater Swimmers School in Key West Florida in 1963. On the first day of the School, a Navy Chief screamed out to the 110 of us students "Only the strong will survive!"

There we did numerous day and night time

swims, but these were all done underwater while wearing a mask, tanks, and swim fins and we only used the breast and side strokes. Although there was a lot of pressure to complete the course, occasionally there was a little humor. Just before entering the water on a difficult night swim, one of the students said, "I am not afraid of sharks, but I can't bear a cuda!" The school was physically demanding to say the least. Of the 110 who started the course only 73 graduated. I was one of the graduates, but then again that was 14 years ago.

The last and biggest thing on the negative scale was that I was going to be attempting all three of these grueling events in a single day, which was totally mind boggling and almost unbelievable.

On the positive side of the scale was the

fact that I was a Marine and had trained and graduated from some of the hardest schools in the military including Army Ranger School, and the Marine Corps Mountain Climbing School, which I finished with a broken arm. These schools were not for the faint of heart, with the mantra being "You either hacked it or you packed it!"

Another huge motivational factor for me was that I had recently read Norman Vincent Peale's book, "*The Power of Positive Thinking*". The book was loaded with a number of amazing examples of what a human being could accomplish with a "Can Do" positive attitude. With the right mental attitude, I knew there was nothing I could not accomplish if I set my mind to it and I was willing to pay the price. I made my decision and "I was in for a penny, in for a pound." Making the decision to do the triathlon took a huge weight off my mind. I was going to "shoot for the moon, and if I missed I'd still be among the stars."

I told Dave Orlowski that I had decided to do the triathlon and the next day he told me that both he and Cpl. Lloyd were in too. I called John Collins and informed him that the three of us were going to compete in the triathlon, along with Marine Gunnery Sergeant Henry Forrest who was stationed at Camp Smith on the other side of the island. John accepted the news with great enthusiasm. John's wild idea had now become a reality for me.

Although there was very little advance publicity about the event, John did create a flyer that got some limited distribution, and a few local radio jockeys had given it a plug or two.

The flyer was titled "First Annual Hawaiian Iron Man Triathlon 0700, 18 February 1978." (see page 61). When I received my copy of the flyer, I thought that John was being pretty ambitious calling it the "First Annual Triathlon," considering the fact that we were not sure if anyone could complete the three events in a single day. John had also given each of us an official entry form which started with the words, "I hereby apply for membership in the "Iron Man Triathlon Organizing Committee…". Along with the entry form, there were two pages of information regarding the rules to the race, as well as a map of the bike course. Upon reading the information, I found it a little unusual that on the bike course that a bicycle, tricycle, skateboard, or any other form of purely human powered locomotion would be allowed. The entry fee to the race was $5.00 (five dollars), and it was to be used to cover the expenses. (see page 59 for the actual copy of my check).

John did a great job putting all of this information together as well as getting a permit to legally conduct the open ocean swim.

As John continued with the myriad of details in getting the triathlon organized, he had hopes of getting somewhere between twenty and forty competitors, including his wife Judy. As it turned out, the twenty figure would be pretty close. I had orders for a thirteen month tour of duty in Okinawa in 1978, and GySgt Henry Forrest was in the same situation with orders for a tour of duty on the mainland in the spring of 1978. John seeing the possible decline in competitors made a command decision. The triathlon would take place on 18 February 1978.

When I look back on the decision to do the triathlon, I often think about the famous quote from Robert Frost when he wrote "***Two roads diverged in a wood and I- - I took the one less traveled by, and it has made all the difference***". The difference here was the fact that this Iron Man triathlon idea was a "road" that had NEVER before been traveled on by anyone in the WORLD!

CHAPTER 3

TRAINING & MORE TRAINING

Knowing that the race was less than two months away, I knew I had little time for anything except training, working, and sleeping. In all the excitement to committing to do the triathlon, I realized the one thing that I had forgotten was the fact I did not have a bike, and that was something which had to be taken care of immediately! After a quick trip down to the Sears & Roebuck department store, and $96 dollars later, I was now the proud owner of a red Free Spirit 3-speed bike which I named "Big Red". Soon my gluteus maximus and the bike seat became very close friends!

Each training day always began with at least one cup of coffee, "The Ambrosia of the Gods". To me, a day without coffee is like a day without sunshine. From Monday through Friday I would get out around 5 a.m. for a quick 7-8 mile run prior to going to work. During which times I enjoyed catching some of the most beautiful sunrises. From there I would clean up and head in to work without stopping for breakfast. It really felt great getting in this early mileage.

At noon, instead of lunch I would run a brisk 8-10 miles with the "Jock for Lunch Bunch". After that there was only time for a quick shower and then rush back to work. Sometimes, even after the shower I was still sweating.

Any time during the work day when I had to travel anywhere on the base, "Big Red" was my faithful companion. When the work day was over I would then bike down a few miles to Lani Kai Beach Park. There were two large buoys anchored a good distance apart in the water and I would swim back and forth between them for 80-90 minutes. After that I would then ride back to the barracks on base. After a quick shower, I would then eat a sandwich or for that matter anything else that was in the refrigerator, and then I would hop in bed to try to get some much needed sleep. One would think that would come easy. That was not always the case, and on numerous occasions I would find it hard to sleep. I was still fired up and my motivational engine was running in high gear knowing the triathlon was another day closer.

The only difference between the workweek and the weekends was the increase in running, swimming and biking mileage on Saturdays and Sundays. My social life dipped down to the near zero level except for the one occasion when Sgt. Major Irrera called me at work on a Friday afternoon and said "Knoll, you don't need to kill yourself with all this daily triathlon training, take a break and lets go to the Staff NCO Club for happy hour." For sure I was more than up for that.

In the motivational area I was re-reading *The Power of Positive Thinking* book and absorbing a lot of the positive thoughts to pump me up. In the physical area I was feeling great, but with this continuous demanding daily regimen I was mentally looking forward to the day we would do the triathlon and get it over with one way or the other. I would either be finishing it, or going down in flames trying. There were no other options!

CHAPTER 4
THE COUNT DOWN

A few days before the event, and with the training being complete for all practical purposes, I began a self assessment of my readiness for the triathlon. The training had gone well, especially considering the brief period I had to train for all three events. It seemed like it was only a few nights ago that John Collins had made his brief announcement about the triathlon, with words worthy to be etched in stone "*anyone who finishes all three events will be an Iron Man and will have bragging rights for the rest of their lives.*"

I was more focused on the "finishing" portion of John's announcement, than the "bragging rights" piece. Being from Wisconsin, and a huge Green Bay Packers fan, I started incorporating some quotes from Coach Vince Lombardi into my mantra. My favorite one was "***Winning isn't everything, it's the only thing!***" Not knowing, but hoping all participants could cross the finish line in less than 24 hours, I changed the mantra to "***FINISHING ISN'T EVERYTHING, ITS THE ONLY THING!***"

Mentally I went over all the training I had accomplished in each 24 hour day. I was on target, but work and sleep jealously wanted their share of the day.

My swim training had gone well, with most of it being done using either the breast stroke, or side stroke which I was very comfortable with. Although the swim portion of the event was going to be the shortest, I knew it was going to be the most challenging for me. If you ran out of "gas" on the bike, the worst thing was that you could fall off of it. If you ran out of "gas" on the run, the worst thing could be falling over from fatigue. Running out of "gas" during the swim, where there are large fish that wear gray suits, was NOT something I cared to dwell on. Enough said on that. One must know one's strengths and weaknesses. My game plan for the swim would be to take it easy and finish. Once back on terra firma, I hoped I would be in good shape for the events to follow and keep heading onward to destiny.

Although I did not know all of the other 14 athletes who would be competing, I did know that some of them had very impressive athletic credentials and one was almost in the professional athlete category. Embarking on the journey into the untried and unknown, I knew there would be a big difference in the level of fitness between those at the front of the pack in contrast to those at the back. Part of the difference was that a few of the participants had the luxury of being able to train almost full time before the event. In contrast, Frank Day, who was a Naval Officer, had only heard about the triathlon two weeks before the event and had signed up. He liked the idea of competing, so to make sure he was ready he did a one mile swim to see if he felt capable of doing the 2.4 mile swim without drowning. He felt that he was, and I felt that if he could finish this, he deserved a trophy for the most Herculean effort!

Between riding my bike everywhere on the air base, and doing the long rides over the weekend, it was apparent that my "okole", which in Hawaiian means "rear end", and my bike seat on "Big Red" for sure were the closest of friends!

As far as the run portion of my training, I felt that it could be characterized as "excellent to outstanding". Besides all the runs I got in during the workweek, I had also done longer runs and races with the Mid Pacific Road Runners Club as well as completing the Honolulu Marathon. The bottom line was that I was as ready as I would get. If you have ever watched a NASA space launch in the final T-Minus 10 count down, I was in that area for the triathlon and I was ready for launch!

CHAPTER 5
THE BIG DAY

Before I knew it, 18 February 1978 had arrived. In the early morning darkness, Marine Cpl. Rex Allen pulled up in a green military issue van to pick me and "Big Red" up. It was 0530 hours, and I had already had a couple of cups of coffee. I was fired up and ready to go. Rex had volunteered to play the role of support crew for Cpl. Dave Orlowski, Cpl. John Lloyd, and myself. Knowingly fully that this could potentially be a 24 hour duty assignment, we were glad to have Rex on board as an important part of our Team. Dave and John were going to meet us on the other side of the island where the swim start would take place at San Souci Beach, which was adjacent to Kapiolani Park.

All of our gear including the bikes were stowed in the van. As we drove across the island, Rex and I were having an exciting conversation about the mind boggling day that was ahead of us. It then got silent, and I worked on mentally getting in to the "zone" and got really pumped up. By the time we arrived at San Souci Beach, I felt as though I could run straight through a brick wall. It doesn't get much better than that. There was no wind and the water was calm. I knew if I could make it through the swim, after that I would be on terra firma for the bike portion and hopefully the run.

It was now 0600 hours, and we had plenty

of time to get ready before attending the mandatory pre-race safety briefing from John Collins.

We all gathered down at the shore, and you could really sense the excitement in the air. We were pioneers getting ready to embark on an adventure to do something that no one else in the world had ever done. Although I knew most of the other 14 participants, there were some that I had never met before. There were also surf board paddlers, a few spectators, and three athletes who had changed their minds about doing the event. Judy Collins, John's wife was also there, but today she would not be competing due to illness. As the intensity level rose, we were all walking around shaking each others hands and having upbeat jovial conversations.

At 0630 hours, John began the safety briefing. (see page 62) In it he told us that we would have to follow all of the traffic signals and not violate any local laws or ordinances. We were all personally responsible for our own physical condition and actions during the event. Someone with an odd sense of humor commented, “If no one gets killed this year, maybe there will be another Iron Man event next year, possibly with a relay category!”

John had answered all of my prayers with the requirement that each of us had to furnish our own surfboard paddler escort for the swim whose job it was to notify the escort boat if a swimmer ran in to problems. Jamie Neely, a fellow runner, was going to be my escort for the 2.4 mile swim. There was a gentlemen’s agreement in place, whereby if you touched the surfboard for any reason you would disqualify yourself from the event.

After the briefing concluded, the anticipation and excitement level was to the point where it could probably be measured high on the Richter Scale. It was *el momento verdad*, the moment of truth. We were now at the T-Minus one second point on the shore, and then John said "GO", and the 15 of us launched into the water, and it was ON!

"Ours was not to question why? Ours was but to do or die!"

It would be a quick test. Do all three events in less than 24 hours. You either pass or you fail. Although we started off as a group, it was not long before the faster swimmers were out of sight. I was doing the breast stroke and side stroke and the "speed" word was not in my mental vocabulary, instead I was using my "LSD" approach (Long Slow Distance). Jamie was staying close by on the surfboard, and continually keeping me pumped up with words of encouragement. Very early on in the swim, I started to have a MAJOR problem - the small pair of goggles I was wearing kept leaking seawater into my eyes. After numerous attempts at trying to clear them, I realized that they were more of a problem than they were worth. Considering them now to be excess baggage, I dedicated them to Davy Jones' Locker and the briny deep. I think my surfboard paddler found this to be quite humorous.

Using the breast stroke and side stroke I was able to keep my eyes out of the water for the most part, but I knew for sure there was going to be a price paid in the eyeball area after 2.4 miles of this. Digging in to the positive mental basket, I decided to charge on!

The swim was going well and I was feeling good. Slowly but surely I was grinding out mileage. Speed was not part of my game plan, but rather just to safely complete the swim. It was great having Jamie with me, as we chatted back and forth positive thoughts to each other.

Using land navigation experience that I had learned during my five years in Recon, combined with my numerous runs along Waikiki, I was able to get a good sense of how far along in the swim I was getting. I could see Waikiki Beach off in the distance, and some early bird surfers beginning to appear. Just before I got up to the pink Royal Hawaiian

Hotel, which was easy to spot, I knew I was now past the one mile mark in the swim. Still feeling great and not caring about how much time had elapsed, I continued following my game plan, which was "just finish the swim."

As I swam along, I was following the sage advice of Dr. Jack Scaff, the head of the Honolulu Marathon Clinic. He said periodically to do a mental check of your body, and from head to toe I was feeling great. Jamie continued to provide encouraging support, and I was now about 1.5 miles in to the swim. I knew for sure that I was in last place. "So what" I told myself, I am still in the arena, and the lions hadn't gotten to me yet! Nor had any of those big fish in gray suits! Thank you Lord for the huge favors! With the two mile mark nearby, Jamie and I were joined by the people on the safety boat, who were cheering and shouting words of encouragement. I shouted back a few times, "I'm going to make it!" The positive thinking was in high gear and I was excited as a kid on Christmas morning. A short time later I was not sure if I was seeing an illusion or the channel buoy marker. As I got closer it was clear that it was indeed the buoy maker and that I had now completed over two miles of the ocean swim. All the many hours of training were now paying off! Getting to the buoy marker I made the required 90 degree turn. It should now be easy finishing the swim to the beach. Not so! I had been forewarned that at this time of the morning the water in the channel would be flowing out to sea, so it was imperative to get out of the channel as quickly as possible. Now I was in the channel and swimming with all the strength I had, but was not progressing. In fact, it seemed like I was moving backwards. I recalled studying one of the laws of relativity. "For every action, there is a reaction." I was getting the reaction. Quickly I did a 90 degree turn out of the channel and then headed back toward the beach sliding over some coral en route.

I finally arrived at the beach, where I was cheered on by a few friends of mine who had been watching over my bike. My finishing swim time was 2:13:05. I knew there was going to be a price to pay for ditching the goggles, and there was. My eyes were burning and they were probably as red as two maraschino cherries! After emerging from the Pacific, I quickly ran through a nearby shower and tried to rinse off the salt and flush out my eyes. From there I threw on a t-shirt and a pair of running shoes and it was off for the 112 mile bike venture. Finding my bike was not going to be a problem, as it was the only one left on the beach and was lying in the sand.

Everyone had successfully completed the swim. Coming out of the water in last place, it was time for either a pity party or to turn on some more of that positive thinking. I chose the latter. "I'm in last place. Great! I can't go down any farther. There is only one way to go now and that is up!

At that time I didn't know that Archie Hapai was out of the water in fifty seven minutes and thirty five seconds, and if he was doing well on the bike he probably was already thirty five miles ahead of me on the bike course. No problem, my first goal now was to hunt down whoever was in 14th place. I had fourteen targets ahead of me to shoot at. Charge!!

About 10 miles into the ride while going up a slight incline on the road which was bordering the beach and the ocean someone in a vehicle behind me was blowing their horn and they were waving me to pull over. It was my friends Gordon and Barbara Dugan who were a few of the folks on the beach when I finished the swim. Gordon said it looked like my bike seat was too low and my legs were not getting a full extension on the downward stroke of the pedals. So we raised the seat some and I was back on my way in high spirits.

There had been virtually no publicity on the triathlon, that it was being held today, and being a Saturday there was a lot of heavy traffic on the highway. Every so often a car would go by and someone would shout some four letter expletives to get off the road. On these occasions some riding in the off road sand and gravel had to be done. The inevitable was bound to happen. I ended up with a flat tire. Rex in the support vehicle was assisting Dave, John, and me and we were spread out by a whole lot of miles. Rex was doing a great job providing support for all three of us as best possible. I dragged the bike under a shady palm tree and waited for Rex to pass by. He arrived about 20 minutes later. It only took a short time to get the tire fixed and I was back on the road pounding the pedals. Somewhere around the 60 mile mark it was time to head up a very long incline to the Schofield Barracks area. The sun was at its zenith and it made me think of the line in Rudyard Kipling's poem Gunga Din. "*The heat would make your blooming' eyebrows crawl.*"

I was expending a lot of energy pumping up this incline so I decided to get off the bike and push the bike up this what was now looking more like a steep hill than an incline. Rex arrived shortly thereafter with an energy drink, an orange. and a couple of pieces of peppermint candy. So while this was working rather well I decided it was time for the orange. It tasted good but some of the juice was now running down my arms and out of nowhere a bunch of flies joined me for the ascent to the top. For sure it was a good workout and it made me think of my premise on hills - the degree of difficulty is in direct proportion to the fatigue of the body.

I had heard that after a short flat portion by the Schofield Barracks there would be a nice downhill stretch. The information was correct and a whole lot more than I had anticipated. I started down this decline and before I knew it I felt that I was in the mach 1 speed range. It was one of the times, Rex in the support vehicle was right along side of me and I heard him scream to me "You're going almost 50 miles per hour". I was hanging on for dear life and my eyes were as large as silver dollars. I didn't want to hit the brakes because I thought it might cause the bike to shimmy. I knew if I fell off the bike there would be a couple hundred yards of scorched skin and a lot of red stuff on the road. It was time to think positive, so I just let it go and rode it out. For sure I had one heck of a ride to the bottom of the hill. I think my bike "Big Red" was saying, "Just hold on, we're going for the gold or we are going to the hospital!" All went well although my fingerprints probably remained in the handle bars for the life of the bike.

Soon I was passing through the Pearl Harbor area, passing by the airport and finishing this part of the triathlon at Aloha Tower in downtown Honolulu. As I got off the bike seat it seemed like I was pulling a plunger off of something. It was time to rack my bike and thank "Big Red" for getting me successfully through the bike portion of the triathlon. With the swim and bike events now complete it was two down and one to go. It was now time for my favorite event, the 26.2 mile marathon.

John Collins' wife, Judy, and a few others were in an air conditioned van at this transition point where they recorded my bike time. If I would have continued right on, my transition time from bike to run would have been about 10 seconds as I already had on my running shoes. Judy felt like John was not that far behind me and if I waited for him, we could run the marathon together. That sounded O.K., but after waiting for more than 15 minutes I became concerned that my muscles might tighten up and that would be no way to start the marathon.

So I took off and I was real pumped up with the swim and the bike portions completed. Soon I was passing through the Waikiki Beach area and feeling great, but I was encountering a lot of traffic, traffic lights, and stop signs forcing me to make periodic stops. I was concentrating a lot on keeping my pace as smooth as possible. We were on the Honolulu Marathon course where that marathon is run every December. Having done many, many miles of training on the course and having run this marathon several times, I think I could have run it blindfolded. Once I reached the Diamond Head area, the traffic and the amount of traffic lights dissipated. The miles were going by smoothly, but I still had hours of running to do and for sure I didn't want to do anything stupid.

If any of us would finish, it would probably be after the sun had set. Once again I was doing a mental check of my body. In NASA vernacular I was "A-OK, Green and Go, with all units functioning." For practically all of us the main goal was to finish all three events in less than 24 hours. I really didn't feel that we were competing that much against each other. Having said that, if anyone finished there would be a pecking order on how we had done, so everyone was giving it their all. We were all doing something that no one in the world had ever done before. Once again, we dared to dream awake dreams that mortals had never dreamed before. I was in orbit looking forward to the successful splash down. All of this was making the miles go by comfortably. In the dark out on the Kalanianaole Highway, I was on a high singing a few songs from the early 1950's. For sure I was in the zone thinking of an old Marine Corps saying: "No task too difficult; no job to great; the difficult we do immediately; the impossible takes a little bit longer." My goal - The Power of Positive Thinking - was to erase the "I" and the "M" from the word "IMPOSSIBLE."! These were truly golden moments out there in the dark. I couldn't imagine I was having all this excitement for five dollars!

A few more miles went by and I passed the 15 mile mark. I was having a real smooth run but there was still 11.2 miles to go. I passed some of my fellow competitors, including Henry Forrest, and I told him to hang in there and make it to the finish line. My training was paying off, a reward for all the hours and hours I had put in it. I was doing some mental chants that I got from Gordon Haller: "*when the going gets tough, the tough get going*", "*if it was easy, anyone could do it*"; and lastly "*I knew the job was risky when I volunteered*".

Elsewhere on the course, history was being made. John Dunbar and Gordon Haller had been exchanging the lead between mile 17 and 21 on the run. John had become dehydrated, as his support crew had run out of water and they gave John some beer. Soon after, he became disoriented and Gordon pulled away running the last five miles in an amazing 31 minutes becoming the first Iron Man in history! Thirty three minutes later, John made it to the finish line to place second overall in the triathlon.

Back to my race..

After a few more miles I passed the 20 mile mark, I really was excited how well everything was going. Again I was also doing a positive mental body check, feet, legs, hips, arms, everything felt great! I knew I was having a good run, but I still was being careful. One of my mottos was "*its not how fast you run the first mile, it's how well you do the last one*". Somewhere around the 21 mile mark, I saw a couple of folks standing along the side of the highway loudly cheering me on. It had been a long day and these were my first cheers of encouragement. I heard someone shout "patience is a virtue", and it was Marine Lieutenant Fran Wilson. She was yelling "Keep it up Marine! You look great!" This was a great energy pump filling up my motivation tank. I was feeling more and more like I would feel the thrill of victory.

Soon I was running up the incline on Diamond Head road. After a short distance the road turned in to a flat area where there was a nice downhill portion as I neared the 25 mile marker.

I almost had to pinch myself to believe that this was all happening. I recalled some people saying that we all were insane. Now I realized that it only seemed insane because no one had ever done it before. I didn't know then that someday millions of people would probably agree with me.

After another mile or so, I finally crossed the finish line of the Honolulu Marathon at Kapiolani Park, where there was a very small group giving me a nice cheer. I was elated that all the hours and hours of training had paid off. I had achieved my goal of finishing and I was now an IRON MAN!

Photo 1 - Marine competitors to be supported by Rex in the Event.

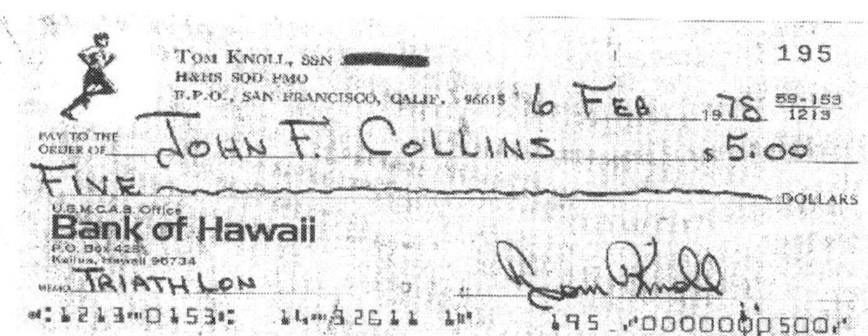
TOM KNOLL, SSN

H&HS SQD PMO

F.P.O., SAN FRANCISCO, CALIF. 96615

195

6 FEB 1978

59-153
1213

PAY TO THE ORDER OF JOHN F. COLLINS $ 5.00

FIVE DOLLARS

U.S.M.C.A.S. Office

Bank of Hawaii

P.O. Box 428

Kailua, Hawaii 96734

MEMO TRIATHLON

Photo 2 - My original check paying the entry fee for the Event.

Photo 3 - Tom Knoll, Dave Orlowski, & John Lloyd early Race Day Morning in front of their race support vehicle.

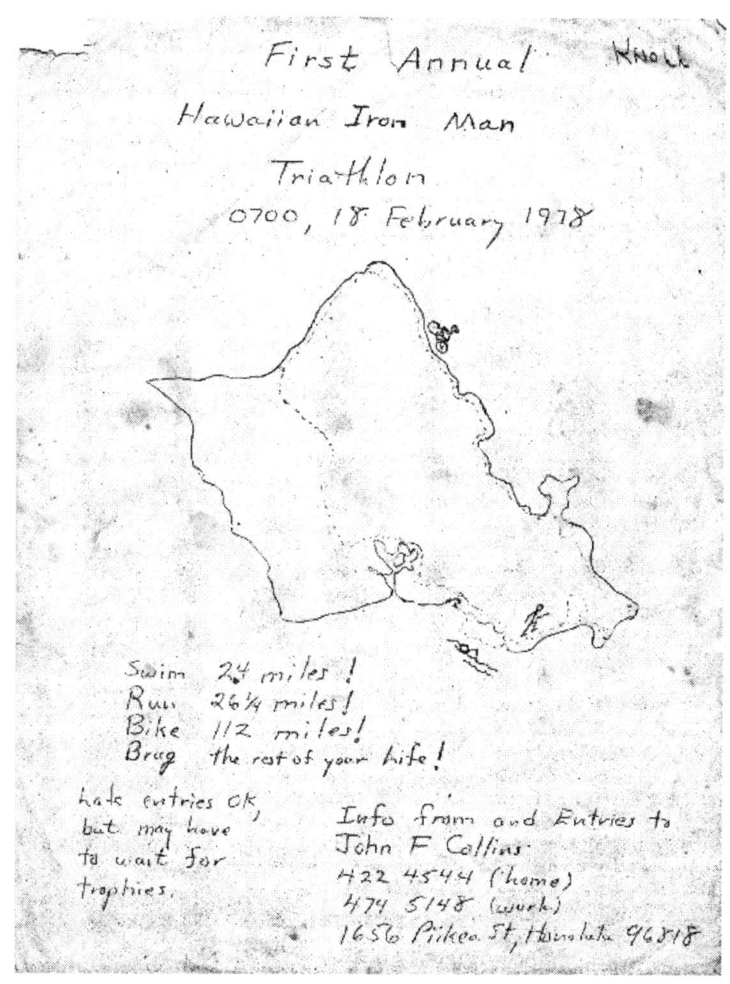

Photo 4 - Original race flyer from 1978.

Photo 5 - John Collins conducting the race-day safety briefing on the beach with his fellow competitors.

Photo 6 - The author and cheering fans (note the soon to be infamous goggles on my head).

Photo 7 - Swim safety paddlers and competitors moments before the swim start.

Photo 8 - The swim start of the First Annual Hawaiian Iron Man Triathlon.

Photo 9 - Dave Orlowski finishing the swim with a time of 1:09:15.

Photo 10 - The author finishing the swim.

Photo 11 - A competitor on the 112-mile bike course.

Photo 12 - Fueling up at the support vehicle.

Photo 13 - Competitors running the 26.2-mile marathon course on race day.

1978 HAWAII IRONMAN TRIATHLON (OAHU, HAWAII)

	SWIM	BIKE	RUN	TOTAL
1st GORDON HALLER	1:20:40	6:56:00	3:30:00	11:46:40
2nd JOHN DUNBAR	1:00:15	7:04:00	4:03:00	12:20:27
3rd DAVE ORLOWSKI	1:09:15	7:51:00	4:59:00	13:59:15
4th IAN EMBERSON	1:01:40	7:47:00	5:15:00	14:03:55
5th STERLING LEWIS	1:02:30	7:47:00	5:15:00	14:04:30
6th TOM KNOLL	2:13:05	8:19:00	4:13:00	14:41:11
7th HENRY FORREST	1:36:42	8:47:00	5:06:00	15:30:11
8th FRANK DAY	1:44:20	8:45:00	6:09:00	16:38:29
9th JOHN COLLINS	1:31:15	9:15:00	6:14:00	17:00:29
10th ARCHIE HAPAI	57:35	8:06:00	8:20:00	17:25:01
11th DAN HENDRICKSON	1:35:35	11:39:00	6:48:00	20:03:28
12th HAROLD IRVING	1:05:30	11:04:00	8:08:00	21:00:30

Photo 14 - Official race results and making history.

Photo 15 - The author's original screen-printed Finishers Shirt from 1978.

Photo 16 - A favorite cartoon of the author.

Photo 17 - The author, still running strong many miles and decades later.

CHAPTER 6
RACE DAY FACTS

Dave Orlowski had a swimming and running background. He had done only one 50-km training bike ride prior to the race. During the course of the run, Dave made a stop at McDonalds for a hamburger, French fries, and a milkshake. He also bought along the way bananas, chocolate bars, etc. Although he had to walk a portion of the marathon, he finished in third place.

John Collins, somewhere during the course of the race, stopped for a bowl of chili.

Somewhere during the course of the bike portion, Frank Day came alongside Henry Forrest, who was having a problem shifting the gears on his bike for a better speed, and helped Henry out.

Frank made a stop during the running portion in Hawaii Kai and drank a large cup of soda and enjoyed a 10 to 15 minute break. He did quite a bit of walking on the marathon course.

Ian Emberson and Sterling Lewis had a near photo-line finish, with Ian edging Sterling by 35 seconds (14:03:55 to 14:04:30).

Archie Hapai and Ian Emberson were competing in the 1978 Iron Man as a prelude to their ultimate goal—to break the world's record for swimming the Molokai channel.

(Unfortunately they were unsuccessful in their record-breaking attempt.)

I guess I might have won the low-calorie award, with a peanut-butter and jelly sandwich, two granola-type bars, an orange, and some peppermint candy as my only nutrition during the race.

John King's race day, for all practical purposes, was over when a car smashed into his bike in dangerous, heavy traffic on the highway. Fortunately he was not seriously injured.

John Lloyd gave it one heck of a try, but somewhere around the 18 to 20 mile mark of the run, he had to drop out, and his race day was finished.

Ralph Yuwata, in an interview, said, "I was

the first official Iron Man dropout." But for sure, it was not because he was not capable of finishing. Ralph and Butch Irving were sharing a support vehicle, just like Dave Orlowski, John Lloyd, and I were doing. Their escort "gave up", and with it being too dangerous to proceed without an escort, Ralph offered to get his car and he accompanied Butch through the rest of the race. Ralph, some of us became Iron Men on this day, but for sure you won the Iron Heart award. You are one hell of a guy.

Dan Hendrickson's flat tire put his race on hold for 90 minutes while he waited for his support vehicle ended up with a finishing time of 20:03:38. You toughed it out, and had a good day, no pun intended. You are an Iron Man, and so is Butch Irving, who was right behind you, at 21:00:30. You got your money's worth out of your $5 entry fee. Great!

CHAPTER 7

POST RACE

One of my mottos has always been that where there is a real challenge there will always be blood, sweat, and tears. Nothing could have proven to be truer than on the day of the triathlon. Crossing the coral reef caused me to bleed, biking and running caused me to sweat, and finally crossing the finish line brought tears of joy to my eyes! I cannot even begin to tell you what it was like to have accomplished an impossible dream!

Harold "Butch" Irving was the final

competitor to cross the finish line and the history of the first Iron Man triathlon was complete and the legend was born. There were fifteen starters and twelve finishers. Let me say something about John Lloyd, Ralph Yawata, and John King. They deserve, and get the well earned respect of all of us who did finish. You competed, gave it all you had and are a part of the history of the First 1978 Iron Man triathlon. Godspeed to all of you! Thanks for being out there with all of us. A few days later we had a small post race party and awards ceremony at the home of the John and Judy Collins. Libations flowed and pu pu's (appetizers) were graciously consumed by all in attendance. John gave each of us a $2.00 refund of our entry fee, as the race had come in under budget. John had told all of us to bring blank t-shirts, or sweat shirts to the gathering. Not long after arriving, we began silk screening the shirts with a design which John had created for the occasion. The design included a robot built out of metal running inside of a triangle with the words "Hawaiian Iron Man Finisher" on the outside. To dry the ink on the shirts we had to place them one at a time on to a pizza board and into the oven in John and Judy's kitchen. To conclude the celebration, John presented each of us with a hand made trophy (see book cover) which he built for us out of parts from the Pearl Harbor shipyard where he was a Navy Commander. The trophy had the figurine of a man made out of metal with a five sided nut for a head mounted on a wooden base with a plate inscribed with the words:

Finisher

1978 Hawaiian Iron Man Triathlon

2.4 Mile Swim 112 Mile Bike Ride 26.2 Mile Run

The nut which formed the head had a hole in it, and it signified that we must have had a "hole in our head" to even think about doing it! Nothing could have been any more true!

I have been offered unbelievable amounts of money for my trophy, but it is

NOT FOR SALE AT ANY PRICE!

CHAPTER 8

THEN & NOW

The following is some information from the 1978 Iron Man and the changes that have taken place through the years up to the present (2013). To try to include everything would be voluminous. The changes that I am including are not in any specific order.

Changes

There were 15 athletes at the start; no women or challenged athletes. Now there are around 2,000 male, female, and challenged competitors.

There were no pre-qualifying requirements to compete in 1978. Now you have to pre-qualify to be able to compete in Kona.

From September 9th, 2012, to August 25th, 2013, there were 32 70.3 and full Ironman qualifying races throughout the world.

All 12 originals were amateurs, and there was no prize purse. There is now a male-female professional division, with each first male and female professional finisher receiving $120,000.

In 1978, each athlete paid a $5 entry fee. In 2013 at Kona, the entry fee was $775.

No helmets were required for the bike portion in 1978, and at least three athletes had bikes that cost less than $100. Now you can spend in excess of $10,000 for a top-of-the-line bike and over $100 for a good helmet.

In 1978 there were no sponsors, no aid or medical stations, no cell phones, portable toilets, or traffic control (except for normal traffic lights and stop signs), no transition areas for the swim and bike, no restriction on bike drafting, no volunteers on the bike and run courses, and little to no media coverage. Today, all of the above are well covered. (For example, in 2013, at Kona, there were over 5,000 volunteers involved.)

An interesting thing in 1978 was each athlete needed to have a support vehicle to take care of anything they might need during the bike-run portion of the event. In one case, two people shared a support vehicle, and in another, three people were supported by the same support vehicle. For the swim, each person was required a have a paddler on a surfboard for safety precautions. Nowadays there are many paddlers and safety boats.

Although in 1978 John Collins gave a short safety brief just before the swim, it was nothing like it in 2013 in Kona. There were mandatory pre-race briefings for the German and Japanese-speaking athletes, a physically-challenged athlete meeting, and a mandatory pre-race briefing for the athletes.

In 1978 there was no media on the day of the race. Now folks like Mike Reilly, the Voice of Ironman, calls out each person's name and states, "You are an Ironman!" when they cross the finish line. Local, national, and international coverage is huge. In 2013 in Kona, Greg Welch, and his crew, handled the TV portion of the race, which gets a huge viewing audience.

About a month after Kona, there is an Ironman World Championship telecast for about 90 minutes. It is viewed by an amazing amount of people around the world.

Today Ironman events make money for charities in the areas where they are being put on. In addition, Ironman has become a multi-million dollar business, benefiting communities, hotels, airlines, restaurants and the producers of Ironman-branded products.

In 2000, in the Olympic Games in Sydney, Australia, the triathlon became an Olympic event. The distances are much shorter with the distances being a 1.5 km (0.93 mi) swim, 40 km (25 mi) cycle, and a 10 km (6.2 mi) run.

Since 1978 vast improvements have been made for those who want to compete in an

Ironman event. Now there are coaches, trainers, triathlon training groups/clubs, books and triathlete magazines to assist athletes, and devices such as PowerCranks and AeroBars to improve bike performances.

In 1978 the goal was to do the swim, bike, and run events in less than 24 hours. In Kona, 73-year old Walt Stack set a record that can't be broken. He completed the race in 26 hours and 20 minutes. Thereafter, in 1982, a time limit was instituted that the entire race must be completed in less than 17 hours.

There are many, many more changes, too numerous to mention.

CHAPTER 9
IN MEMORIAM
OF HENRY FORREST

Henry C. Forrest, Gunnery Sergeant, USMC, completed the 1978 Hawaii Iron Man Triathlon in seventh place. He would compete again in 1979, 1980, 1982, 1988, and 2004.

In August 2007, Henry was diagnosed with pancreatic cancer, which began to sap the strength of this dynamic person, but not his determined, amazing, can-do attitude.

On July 4, 2008, the 3,000-plus mile

Freedom Charity Run from San Diego to Washington, D.C., that my son, Warren, and I were doing was almost completed, with a little over a quarter of a mile to the finish at the Marine Corps Iwo Jima Memorial Monument adjacent to Arlington Cemetery. A lot of friends, including 1978 Ironman Dave Orlowski, were there to welcome us, plus an NBC TV crew.

I was unaware that one of the most exciting moments of the run had yet to occur. With only minutes to go, I glanced to my left and there was Henry Forrest jogging alongside me. I was so excited that I had to stop for a moment to make sure it was really him. He had six stomach tubes, and an IV-bag had to be reattached to him when he was back in his wheel chair after the quarter-mile run. But he gave a sharp Marine Corps salute. Henry had left a hospital bed in Atlanta and was driven to Washington, D.C. by members of his family so that he could join in on the last mile of this cross-USA charity run. He had now accomplished what he came to Washington, D.C. to do.

Having been involved in the Korean conflict, Vietnam, Afghanistan and Iraq, I've had the chance to observe a lot of heroic individuals. But in a non-hostile environment I list Henry's jogging with me in the waning days of his life as one of the most awe-inspiring, "digging down deep" shows of endurance in my first 75 years on this planet, and I figured I would never see something of this magnitude again.

But Henry would prove me wrong, and

many of us got to see that he had one more heroic effort left in the well, showing his incredible stamina and the power of positive thinking. Henry's battle with pancreatic cancer was one we all knew he was losing, but it was one he would not lose easily.

Between 9 and 13 October, 2008, Henry would come up with one last totally amazing Ironman performance. He and his wife Lou joined other 1978 Ironmen John Collins, Frank Day, Dave Orlowski, and myself at Kona for the Ironman World Championship. Along with having the chance to be with all of us, Henry had come to support Orlowski, as Dave competed in his second Ironman competition, his first attempt at Ironman in 30 years.

Henry's oncologist had given him daily IV treatments of electrolytes to build up his strength and had only at the last moment given him permission to make the long trip from Atlanta to Kona.

On the day of the Ironman competition, Henry and I were given permission to be right down at the finish line.

We greeted Marine Major Bill Connor, a multi-time Iraq and Afghanistan veteran. Bill had done the full bike and run phases of the triathlon in Marine combat helmet, desert camouflage trousers, and combat boots. Henry and I gave him a big salute and a bear hug after he crossed the finish line.

Some hours later, Dave Orlowski crossed the finish line. Henry and I gave him a Marine Corps salute, a loud cheer, and a bear hug. Dave told us that he was inspired to keep going despite burnt and blistered feet, when he thought about what Henry had gone through to be at the finish for him.

Chrissie Wellington, the First Place woman's finisher, was down at the finish line greeting finishers. I gave her the details on Henry and she graciously chatted with him. Henry was smiling from ear to ear.

Henry, with health declining rapidly, returned home a few days later to be with his family, and after a few days in home hospice, he passed away on 6 November 2008.

The first of us original 1978 Hawaii Ironman triathletes has now passed through the pearly gates of heaven. Henry, you have definitely raised the bar to an amazing height for the rest of us who will eventually follow you. While now enjoying your golden wings, I know that if there are places in heaven where a person can swim, bike, and run, you will have the first Ironman in the sky ready when the rest of us original 1978 Ironmen join you there. So God Bless You, Semper Fidelis, and rest in peace. In the famous words of Mike Riley, the Voice of Ironman, "YOU ARE AN IRONMAN!"

CHAPTER 10
TRIATHLON
HISTORICALLY SPEAKING

There were three significant precursors to the swim-bike-run event format.

In the decade after World War I, the Honolulu YMCA had an event they called "Plunge, Pedal and Plod," which involved a bicycle segment, followed by a run along the beach and finishing with a swim.

On September 4th, 1921, the Petit Perillon Swim Club in Marseilles, France, held an event they called "Course des Trois Sports," or the

Race of Three Sports. They started with a bicycle leg of about 7 kilometers, then ran 5 kilometers, and finished with a 200 meter out-and-back swim in the Mediterranean. Women were given a head start, and one of them came in first place.

In September 1974, Jack Johnston and Don Shanahan of the San Diego Track Club announced in their newsletter an event headlined "Run, Cycle, Swim – Triathlon Set for the 25th." This was the first time the word "Triathlon" was used in the modern sense.

The event was called the "First Annual? Mission Bay Triathlon" (showing with a sense of humor that they weren't sure the event would be continued). The race consisted of segments of running, bicycle riding, and swimming. There were 6 miles of running, broken up into segments, with the longest continuous stretch being 2.8 miles, 5 miles of bicycle riding, all in one stretch, and 500 yards of swimming, with the longest continuous stretch being 250 yards. Approximately 2 miles of the running was required to be run barefoot over grass and sand.

There were 46 competitors, including John Collins, his wife Judy, and their two children Kristin and Michael.

The engraver who did the plates on our trophies had to ask Cmdr. Collins how to spell the word triathlon, as he could not find it in the dictionary!

CHAPTER 11

WHAT I HAVE BEEN UP TO SINCE 1978

1978 was a pretty big year for me, besides finishing the first Iron Man Triathlon, I set another monumental goal while I was stationed in Okinawa. I decided that I would raise one million dollars for charity. I was inspired to do this after running the perimeter of the island of Okinawa to raise money for crippled children there.

I didn't realize it at the time, but I would later take running ultra distances to raise money for charity to a pretty crazy level. In fact, since 1978 I have done charity runs with distances over three thousand miles. In 2012, at the young age of 79, I ran from New Orleans LA to International Falls MN covering 1,650 miles in 46 days averaging 33 miles per day. This was the first cross USA run that I went South to North across the country, after having already done it twice. My first cross USA run went from Washington D.C. to Los Angeles CA, taking me 64 days, and averaging 46 miles per day. My second cross USA run took me from San Diego CA to Washington D.C..

Most of the time when I haven't been busy running, I have been actively serving our Country since retiring after 33 great years in the Marine Corps in 1983.

Not being one to sit around, I found myself

working over seas with various American intelligence agencies with deployments to Japan, Thailand, and Germany. After the terrorist attacks of 9/11, I found myself again honored at the age of sixty-nine to go fight another war in Iraq and Afghanistan, after already having served as a Marine in Korea and Vietnam. Age is not an excuse to take a rain check when your Country needs you, and I am very proud of the selfless sacrifice that all our men and women in uniform are doing for us. God Bless You.

In 2010, I reached a major mile stone, my goal of raising a million dollars for charity was reached. It is now 2013 and I am working on raising my second million dollars for charity. When in Hawaii, I run with seven other senior citizens and our average age is 86, and our oldest runner is 93 years of age. We meet 0630 hours on Wednesday mornings and run 4-5 miles on many areas on Oahu. Each runner has an interesting bio and an eight page article on us was published in the May 2013 issue of *Runner's World* magazine entitled "The Over The Hill Gang".

CHAPTER 12

EPILOGUE

35 years have passed since the 1978 Hawaii Ironman became history. Flying over to Kona on 8 October 2013, to spend seven days of festivities at the 35th anniversary of the Ironman World Championship, I was already getting excited. But this 35th anniversary was going to be very special. Five of the original Iron Men, John Collins, Gordon Haller, Dave Orlowski, Frank Day, and I, would all be there in Kona, with Gordon Haller and Dave Orlowski competing in the race.

On Thursday, I ran into Paul Huddle, Paula

Newby-Fraser, Rock Fry, in their Underpants Run. It was a huge, wild crowd, with the run making money for various local charities. On Friday afternoon, Gordon Haller, Dave Orlowski, Frank Day and I did a one-hour presentation at Splasher's Restaurant. Indie is the owner and she has adopted all of us original Iron Men, and each year gives us red-carpet treatment. After our talk, there was a photo, autograph, and question-and-answer session. One person said, "I know John Collins and Gordon Haller are in the Ironman Hall of Fame. Now, my question is, why haven't you other ten 1978 triathletes and maybe the other three who gave it their all but didn't quite finish, been inducted in to the Ironman Hall of Fame?" I said, "Good question which is often asked, but I guess only the World Triathlon Corporation has the answer."

So the presentation ended on a very high note. I sold my 3,000th and last copy of my book, "*Why Not a Million*?" None of these copies were sold in stores, so I got to meet and chat with a lot of wonderful people during the years of marketing the book. A lot of the profit went to various charities. It all helped to completing the 1978 goal to make a million dollars-plus for charity, which was completed in 2011.

All of us five originals had received VIP passes for the "E Komo Mai" Welcome Banquet. Along with friends and family, Gordon, Dave, Frank, and I were seated at two tables, with John and Judy Collins seated closer to the stage. There was a great presentation of Hawaiian history with singing, dancing, a lot of drums, and a fire dancer. We were all enjoying the food and beverages with a lot of laughter and jovial conversation.

Andrew Messick, Chief Executive, Ironman, gave a short presentation. In it he introduced John and July Collins as the founders of the 1978 Hawaii Iron Man. There was a nice round of applause. Next Gordon Haller, who was the first place finisher in 1978, was introduced, and all of us, along with everyone else, gave him a hearty round of applause. Next, Andrew Messick indicated that there were a couple of other original 1978 Iron Men in the audience. First he mentioned Dave Orlowski, and we all gave him a cheer. Next he mentioned Michael Collins, apparently not knowing that Michael was not one of the original twelve 1978 Iron Men. I looked at Frank Day and he looked at me. Wow! After the party, Frank and I kiddingly congratulated Michael Collins, as now being one of the original Iron Men. I jokingly said, "I'm not sure which one of us you replaced." Michael, with a great sense of humor, said, "Hey, they were only off by a year and a day," since he had done it the second year. I said, "You're a class act, Mike." Talking later with Frank, I remembered General Douglas MacArthur's speech, in which he said, and I quote, "Old soldiers never die, they just fade away." I looked at Frank smiling, and said, "I guess old Iron Men never die, they just wade away."

Saturday was our raison d'etre, our reason for being here in Kona. It was race day. With the excitement being at a high, fevered pitch, I briefly flashed back to 1978, and 15 of us entering the water with our surfboard handlers, and a few friends and spectators watching. Here with thousands of people lining the seawall and the course, I watched approximately 2,000 male and female professional athletes, and amateurs, enter the water, with a helicopter flying overhead, and Mike Reilly, the Voice of Ironman, going wild. It was totally amazing and mind-boggling for me. Fifteen of us in 1978 had created all this. Mike announced that 80,000 people throughout the world had competed for the chance to be here. I stayed on the course for the whole 17 hours. There was, as always, a huge crowd out there at midnight cheering the last finishers as they came in.

But there was not much time for rest. On Sunday morning I rushed over to Quinn's Restaurant, the Green Bay Packer headquarters on Kona for all their games, for the 8 o'clock kickoff. Twenty Packer fans were there for the game.

In the evening, it was time for the Banquet of Champions, and a lot of us attended. And as it ended, it was time to say to a lot of friends, "Aloha until we meet again."

So here it is time to wrap up the first 35 years of Ironman, and as Bob Hope would have said, "Thanks for the memories." People often ask me, "Don't you want to slow down a bit?" The answer is no. I've really got some big things coming up in 2014. I'm not going to sit back and watch the grass grow and the paint dry.

NOTABLE AWARDS
I HAVE RECEIVED

Member of the Ronald Reagan Running Team

Runner's World Magazine Golden Shoe Award

Government of Japan's Prestigious "Good Deed" Copper Award Medal for Foreigners

Presidential Sports Award

Charities We Proudly Support

www.SunshineFoundation.org

www.SemperFiFund.org

www.WoundedWarriorProject.org

www.ChallengedAthletes.org

www.Rotary.org

www.JimmyV.org